Love Me, Love My Wife

Love Me, Love My Wife

Ten Reasons Christians Must Join a Local Church

CHARLES ERLANDSON

WIPF & STOCK · Eugene, Oregon

LOVE ME, LOVE MY WIFE
Ten Reasons Christians Must Join a Local Church

Copyright © 2020 Charles Erlandson. All rights reserved. Except for brief quotations in critical publications or reviews, no part of this book may be reproduced in any manner without prior written permission from the publisher. Write: Permissions, Wipf and Stock Publishers, 199 W. 8th Ave., Suite 3, Eugene, OR 97401.

Scripture taken from the New King James Version, copyright © 1982 by Thomas Nelson, Inc. Used by permission. All rights reserved.

Wipf & Stock
An Imprint of Wipf and Stock Publishers
199 W. 8th Ave., Suite 3
Eugene, OR 97401

www.wipfandstock.com

PAPERBACK ISBN: 978-1-7252-6629-2
HARDCOVER ISBN: 978-1-7252-6630-8
EBOOK ISBN: 978-1-7252-6631-5

Manufactured in the U.S.A.   04/14/20

Contents

Introduction		vii
Chapter 1	The Church Is the Bride of Jesus Christ	1
Chapter 2	The Church Is the Body of Christ	6
Chapter 3	The Church Is the House of God	10
Chapter 4	The Church Is Your Mother	15
Chapter 5	The Church Is Your Family	19
Chapter 6	You Are Your Tribe	22
Chapter 7	The Bible and the Church Always Go Together	26
Chapter 8	The Church Is Filled with Sinners Just Like You	33
Chapter 9	Don't Excommunicate Yourself	38
Chapter 10	God Commands It!	42
Next Steps		45

Introduction

HAVE YOU EVER THOUGHT that you can know and love God all by yourself and don't really need the church?

Have you ever left a church because you felt it was filled with a bunch of hypocrites?

Good! Then this little book is for you.

Every week I come across a Christian just like you—sometimes more than one.

While I understand why you no longer go to church, I think you're wrong! But don't take my word for it: let's look at what God says in his Word, the Bible. After you're done exploring what the Church is really about and why you should be going, see if what I'm saying makes sense and if it's time for you to act on what you've learned.

This book is also for you if you:

- know someone who thinks he doesn't need to go to church,
- are a pastor or church leader,
- want to know more about why God says the Church is so important.

A WORD ABOUT THE WORD "CHURCH"

Before we begin, let me clarify two things: what the word "church" means and why I'm talking about more than simply "going to church."

INTRODUCTION

"Going to church" is an unfortunate phrase, because being a Christian is not about "going to church"—it's about loving the Church and *being* the Church. And the Church is the Body and Bride of Jesus Christ.

The word "church" has many different meanings today. For example, when you say the word "church," many people will first think of a church building. But the word "church" literally means "congregation," "assembly," or "holy fellowship."

In the Bible, the meaning of the church as a congregation has two related meanings.

First, the church is the local community of believers (see Paul's letters to local churches in cities such as Rome, Ephesus, Philippi, and Colossi).

Second, the Church is the universal community of believers (see Eph 1:22, 3:10, 21; 5:22–32).

To be a member of *the* Church, that is, the one, universal Church that has always existed since the time of Jesus and always will, you need to be a member of a local church. The local church, which many have chosen to leave, is each individual Christian's connection to the one true Church, and, therefore, his connection to God.

In this book, I'll use "church" (lowercase) to mean the local church and "Church" (capitalized) to mean the one, universal Church.

CHAPTER 1

The Church Is the Bride of Jesus Christ

I HAPPEN, BY THE grace of God, to be married to a wonderful wife named Jackie.

God has graced our lives with an amazing union that is a gift from him. We have unity in our religious beliefs, child-training philosophies, love of beautiful creations, frugality, and many other things. Our lives are united and entwined in countless ways. And we practice loving each other, not just with romance, but by doing good things for each other. Love is the superglue that holds us together.

So, you might understand how I would react if someone said to me, "Fr. Charles, I love you. I think you're great. But you've got a real witch for a wife. She's nothing but trouble, and I can't stand to be around her. She's the stupidest, ugliest, most unpleasant person I know, as well as being a hypocrite. I'm happy to talk with you on the phone or text you, but I'll never enter into your house as long as she's there."

Love me, love my wife.

Now in this human analogy, there may actually be times where one spouse is pleasant and nice to hang out with, and the other one is an absolute train wreck.

But this is not the case with God and his Bride, the Church.

For while God is perfect and we all know the Church is not, Jesus Christ has a special relationship with his Bride. This special relationship is what this book is all about and why you need to be an active member of a local church.

But first, a little theology.
Did you know that God has taken a Bride?!
It's true. The story of God and man, which is the story of the Bible, is a love story. It's a story about how God created man to spend the rest of his life in close communion with him. Sadly, as we know, man has divorced himself from God by his sins: this divorce is the source of the hells on earth that we create for ourselves.

We were created for the deepest fellowship with God. In fact, the Bible begins and ends with a wedding!

In the beginning (Genesis 1), the first wedding is that of God and man. But there's also a human marriage at the beginning of the Bible: the marriage of Adam and Eve. When God created Adam, he said of Adam: "It is not good that the man should be alone; I will make him a helper fit for him." And so, God created Eve for Adam.

Moses, the divinely inspired author of Genesis, says: "Therefore a man shall leave his father and his mother and hold fast to his wife, and they shall become one flesh" (Gen 2:24).

In other words, from the beginning, God created men and women to come together and become one flesh. Two people become one person, or relationship, in marriage. A husband and his wife are no longer to live for themselves but for the other: they do this through self-giving love.

Maleness and femaleness in general, and a husband and wife in particular, picture who God is for us. Who is God? He is three Persons—the Father, the Son, and the Holy Spirit—but one God.

For this reason, it is men and women together, and especially husbands and wives, who picture God for us. God has imprinted his very nature on our bodies!

St. Paul explains the relationship between Jesus Christ and the Church in terms of a marriage. In Ephesians 5, Paul writes about how the husband is the head of the wife in the same way that Jesus is the head of the Church. Women are to submit to their husbands, and husbands are to love their wives. Husbands and wives are to love each other as they love their own bodies.

But it turns out that Paul is talking about more than husbands and wives. He says he's talking about Christ and the Church! In verses 31–32 he says, "'For this reason a man shall leave his father and mother and be joined to his wife, and the two shall become one flesh.' This is a great mystery, but I speak concerning Christ and the church."

I told you that the Bible also ends with a marriage, which we find in Revelation 21:1–3, where St. John refers to the Church as the New Jerusalem. He says:

> Now I saw a new heaven and a new earth, for the first heaven and the first earth had passed away. Also there was no more sea. Then I, John, saw the holy city, New Jerusalem, coming down out of heaven from God, prepared as a bride adorned for her husband. And I heard a loud voice from heaven saying, "Behold, the tabernacle of God is with men, and He will dwell with them, and they shall be His people. God Himself will be with them and be their God."

This is where eternal life is going: to a marriage between Jesus Christ and his Bride, the Church.

John also refers to this as the marriage supper of the Lamb (Rev 19:9). Jesus Christ and his wife, the Church, are one.

Therefore, *how you treat the Church is how you are treating Jesus.*

You really can't say "I love God," whom you haven't seen, if you don't love Jesus' Bride, whom you have seen.

It's a good idea to know what Jesus Christ thinks about the Church. Jesus loves his Church. As Paul says in Ephesians 5:25–29:

> Husbands, love your wives, just as Christ also loved the church and gave Himself for her, that He might sanctify and cleanse her with the washing of water by the word,

> that He might present her to Himself a glorious church, not having spot or wrinkle or any such thing, but that she should be holy and without blemish. So husbands ought to love their own wives as their own bodies; he who loves his wife loves himself. For no one ever hated his own flesh, but nourishes and cherishes it, just as the Lord does the church.

Do you see how much Jesus loves his Wife, the Church? He loves her so much that he died for her and continues to give his life for her. Everything he does is to glorify, nourish, and love her.

Jesus sees the Church, his Bride and Body, as he sees himself.

We also know how Jesus feels about his Bride, the Church, from the life of Paul, back when he was Saul. I'm sure you remember the story of how Saul was on the road to Damascus to hunt down Christians and either throw them into prison or have them put to death. On his way, Jesus dramatically comes to him, knocking him down to his feet. Here's how St. Luke describes what happens next:

> Then he fell to the ground, and heard a voice saying to him, "Saul, Saul, why are you persecuting Me?"

And he said, "Who are You, Lord?"

> Then the Lord said, "I am Jesus, whom you are persecuting." (Acts 9:4–5)

Did you catch what Jesus said to Saul, when Saul asked him who he was? He said, "I am Jesus, whom you are persecuting."

Now how could Saul be persecuting Jesus when Jesus was safely seated at the right hand of the Father, ever since Acts 2? Because Saul was persecuting the Church, which is both the Body of Christ and the Bride of Christ.

Jesus is saying in essence to Saul, "Hurt my wife, and you hurt me. Persecute my wife, and you're persecuting me. Whatever you do to the Church, you're doing to me."

Jesus has so closely identified himself with the Church that he says to all of us, and not just Saul: *"How you treat the Church is how you are treating me."*

JESUS IS NOT A POLYGAMIST

Jesus Christ is not a polygamist!

But this is sometimes, without meaning to, how we think about his relationship with us. Many Christians believe that their relationship with Jesus is primarily an *individual* one. In other words, it's a direct, immediate relationship with Jesus, without any other men or women involved.

Although God does, indeed, relate to each of us individually, this relationship takes place in the context of the larger relationship between Christ and his Bride, the Church.

There are two and a half billion Christians in the world today. Does this mean that Jesus has two and a half billion brides? God forbid! That would make Jesus the ultimate polygamist.

Jesus has one and only one Bride: the Church. Each individual Christian is but one member of this beautiful and holy Bride of Jesus.

Most humans throughout history thought of personality in terms of *corporate personality*. This is true not only for the ancient, medieval, and Reformed world but also for most of the world today.

The Persons of the Trinity are Persons *in relation* to each other. This is most obviously true in terms of the Father and the Son, who are not separate people in the sense with which we often speak of ourselves.

We see this corporate personality in the way that each of us is defined by our *tribe*. When Adam fell, for example, the whole human race fell with him. Why? Because even hundreds of generations later, we're all related to Adam. When Jesus took on a perfect human nature and lived a perfect human life, how is that we can be made holy and perfect in him? Because of corporate personality.

This means that Christians are in, or are a part of, Jesus Christ.

This idea of corporate personality will be made clearer in chapter 2 when we discuss the Church as the Body of Jesus Christ.

CHAPTER 2

The Church Is the Body of Christ

GOD CALLS THE CHURCH not only the Bride of Christ but also the *Body* of Christ.

It's not hard to see why. Remember when we were talking about Adam and Eve how God said that he had made them "one flesh." When a husband and wife marry, they become one flesh, a union sealed and symbolized by sexual union. The husband's body no longer belongs only to him but also to his wife, and the wife's body belongs to her husband and not just to her.

And so, the Church, as the Bride of Jesus Christ, is also the Body of Jesus Christ. The New Testament often speaks of the Church as being *in* Christ and *united* to him. Just as a man and his wife become one thing or person, so do Jesus and his Bride.

This makes sense, since, in Jesus, God and man are made one, or "married."

BODIES AND MEMBERS

The Church as the Body of Jesus Christ is St. Paul's favorite image for expressing the truth of who we are as the Church. Let's look at one important passage where Paul teaches that the Church is the Body of Christ: 1 Corinthians 12. The whole chapter is about how the entire Church is the Body of Christ, but one of the most important verses in the chapter is verse 27, where Paul says: "Now you [plural] are the body of Christ, and members individually."

Paul's point in 1 Corinthians 12 is that each of the members in the Body of Christ is incomplete without all of the other members of the Body. There is only one Body of Christ, not many. Therefore, since the Corinthian Christians are all members of the one Body of Christ, they should live in love and build the Body up, and not use their gifts for selfish gain.

Consider your own body for a moment. What would happen if each part of your body thought it had an independent connection to you? Your brain would be over here, your eyes over there, your ears somewhere different, and everything else all over the place, dismembered from one another.

If this happened to your body, all of the members would die. Each member only has an identity in terms of the larger, greater body, and each member only has life when connected to the body.

Jesus Christ has a Body, of which each individual Christian is to be a member. If you are living as a Christian without being part of the local church, you are like a body part trying to live without being part of the body. In bodies, this leads quickly to death. In the lives of Christians, it leads to spiritual death, but more slowly.

Maybe a simple diagram will help.

Many Christians believe that the relationship between Jesus, the Church, and the individual believer looks like this:

Christ-Christian-Church

In this view, Jesus has a personal and individual relationship with each Christian believer, apart from the Church. The Church is at the end of this relationship and is seen as optional. Since each believer has his own relationship directly with Jesus, he doesn't need the Church. Now he may want it as a devotional aid, something to help him in his personal walk with God, but he doesn't need it.

But the way God portrays the relationship is actually like this:

Christ-Church-Christian

Jesus has established a close, personal union with his Bride and his Body, the Church. Individual Christians are members of

Christ only when they are also members of the Church. Remember: members can only live in relation to the whole body.

When Paul calls the Church the Body of Jesus Christ, he really means it. The Church is his physical, bodily presence on earth.

WHAT IF THE CHURCH WEREN'T THE BODY OF CHRIST

This is really important. Think of what it would mean if the Church were not the Body of Christ. Jesus rose from the dead on Easter Sunday and ascended into heaven forty days later, and then was never seen again, and will not be until the Second Coming.

Doesn't that seem *wrong*?

Wouldn't it be a little anticlimactic if Jesus spent thirty-three years on earth, only three in his public ministry, and then left the earth and was never seen again until the Second Coming? God must have thought that man and even human bodies are really important things for him to take them into himself like he did.

What would Christianity or the world look like if every Christian thought and acted as if he didn't need the Church?

Imagine that all of the following things would be gone forever in a Christianity without the Church.

1. the Lord's Supper
2. corporate worship
3. sermons
4. authoritative teaching of the truth (which would lead to heresy)
5. authoritative teaching on morality
6. churches to help the poor or visit the needy
7. pastors to counsel people or give them spiritual advice
8. discipline or accountability

How effective in glorifying God, establishing his Kingdom, converting unbelievers, ministering to those in need, learning more about

God, and receiving godly guidance and wisdom would Christians be if *none* of them belonged to a local church?

Without any churches, individual Christians would eventually look just like the unbelievers who surround them. Almost all of their "tribes" would be secular, and very few of them, if any, would do much to lead us closer to God.

The Church is the Body of Jesus Christ: it is his eyes and ears, his hands and feet, his voice and his heart. Without the Church, how would men see and know God?

CHAPTER 3

The Church Is the House of God

THE CHURCH IS NOT only the Body and Bride of Christ: it's also the house of God, the place where God lives!

Throughout the Bible, God builds his house (or temple), the place where he intends to live with man. In the beginning, God's house was in the garden in Eden, which was part of the larger world. When God called his people out of Egypt, he told them to build a portable house, the tabernacle. This is the place where he would put his name and his glory and where he would meet with men.

Later, Solomon built the permanent temple, where God lived with his people and where they offered him sacrifices. But the temple was never meant to last forever, and it was destroyed in 70 AD. Does this mean that God no longer has a home on earth? Of course not!

The true temple, according to the New Testament, is Jesus Christ. For the second Person of the Trinity, the Son, took on a human nature, so that God might live with man eternally through Jesus.

Jesus has ascended into heaven, and we can't see him in his body the way his disciples could. Does this mean that God no longer lives with men, or that he only lives in two and a half billion men, women, and children independently?

No! God says that the Church is now the place where he lives with men, and the place where his glory dwells. Knowing what you now know about the Church as the Body and Bride of Christ, this makes a lot of sense.

St. Paul calls the Church, the Body of believers, the temple of the Lord. He does this twice in his first letter to the church at Corinth. First, he says, "Do you not know that you are the temple of God and that the Spirit of God dwells in you?" (3:16). Then, he says, "Or do you not know that your body is the temple of the Holy Spirit who is in you, whom you have from God, and you are not your own?" (1 Cor 6:19).

What most people don't know (because you can't tell by looking at English translations) is that Paul uses the *plural* word for "you" in both passages. It's the Church as a whole that is the temple of the Lord, not just individual believers.

THE CHURCH IS A VISIBLE CHURCH

Sometimes, because the Church is the Body of all Christian believers (and for other reasons), Christians think of the Church as being invisible and that it is not present in visible ways. But this is not right.

Bodies and houses are by their very nature visible and can be seen, felt, and heard. The Church is no different: the Body and temple in which God dwells are visible. In fact, the Church, as the temple of God, shows forth God's glory to the world in many visible ways. And glory is a visible presence or manifestation of something that is glorious.

In the Old Testament, the glory of God was shown especially in the temple. For this reason, its objects were covered with precious metals: gold, silver, and bronze. The temple itself was a large, glorious structure that looked more and more glorious as you progressed into it.

So how is the glory of God's temple shown today? Paul says it's by the Church. He writes: "to Him (God) be glory in the church" (Ephesians 3:21). A little earlier, Paul says that even the angels are taught the wisdom of God by the Church (3:10).

The Church, therefore, is the glorious temple of the Lord, the place where God dwells, and the place where he is revealed to the world. This means that the Church is visible and tangible to the world.

If the Church is the Body and temple of Christ and continues his divine ministry on earth, then the Church must not only be visible but must also have the authority of Christ. This authority can't mean the authority of each individual Christian, and from the book of Genesis to the book of Revelation, God works in groups of his gathered people and their God-appointed leaders.

The Church is the visible temple of God in these ways:

1. The Church has visible, ordained leaders: this is true for the Old Testament, the New Testament, and throughout Church history.
2. These ordained ministers are called to minister in a local, visible body that gathers together for worship on the Lord's Day.
3. It's in the local, visible church that the Word of God is authoritatively preached and taught.
4. Only in the local, visible church are the sacraments present.
5. It's the local, visible church that administers discipline when necessary.
6. It's in the local church that the union of God's people is made visible and the union of God's people with God is made visible.

Bodies and temples are visible things!

The one universal Church is made visible and touchable in each local church.

THE HOUSE OF GOD IS FOR CORPORATE WORSHIP

The house of God, or temple, is also where the people of God worship God together (*corporate worship*). It's on Sunday mornings that the Church as the Body of Christ is most visible. It's easy to forget that you're a Christian or that God is the Lord of your life if you live a life outside the local church. But on Sunday mornings it's visible to all that the local church is the Body of Christ.

When God wanted his people to worship him in the Old Testament, what did he do? He had them build the temple.

The temple was where the priests offered the sacrifices that took away the sins of the people. And all Israelite men were required to come to the temple three times a year to gather together and sacrifice. The temple was built by the people of God, who joyfully brought their gifts of gold, silver, bronze, and precious gems, as well as their animal sacrifices.

It's no different in the New Testament: God has a new and perfect temple, which is the Body of Jesus Christ: not only the natural body of Christ, now ascended into heaven, but also the Church, the Body of Christ.

Peter says in 1 Peter 2:5 that "you also, as living stones, are being built up a spiritual house, a holy priesthood, to offer up spiritual sacrifices acceptable to God through Jesus Christ." Each of us is a stone, and only together are we built up into a spiritual house, which is the Church or temple. No gem, no matter how precious, can say he's the house of God all by himself. Notice as well that it is in the Church as a whole, both as a holy priesthood and as a spiritual house, that the sacrifices of God's people are made.

Paul says the same thing in another way in Ephesians 4:11–12: "And He Himself gave some to be apostles, some prophets, some evangelists, and some pastors and teachers, for the equipping of the saints for the work of ministry, *for the edifying of the body of Christ.*"

Whether as a body or as a house, the Church is built up when each Christian uses his gifts for the good of the local church.

Paul teaches that the gifts of these different ministries are given that together we "may grow up in all things into Him who is the head—Christ—from whom the whole body, joined and knit together by what every joint supplies, according to the effective working by which every part does its share, causes growth of the body for the edifying of itself in love" (Eph 4:15–16).

Paul says a lot of important things in this passage. First, he discusses how the local church has leaders appointed by God. Some people in the local church are leaders, but all Christians are to be members. Second, the reason we have leaders and their gifts, as well as all members and their gifts, is to *edify* the church. To edify means to build up. The purpose of each member of the Church is to bring his gifts and talents into the church so that the church can be built up in love into the image of Christ.

When individual members don't become part of the local church, they rob the church of an important member that God desired to use for the good of all. Notice how Paul says that the members must all work together, which can only happen if each member has joined a local church and faithfully makes his sacrifice there.

What sacrifice? I'll go ahead and say it: God's people are required to tithe or give their money to build up the Church. God gave you your money, and he commands that you give some of it back to build his temple.

But God also requires your gifts and talents. There are many things each local church should do, but one of the reasons she can't do it is because not enough members are actively offering their gifts and talents to God in the Church.

When God told Abraham to sacrifice Isaac, the son of promise, Isaac looked around and wondered where the sacrifice was. Of course, it was him!

In the same way, you might look around and wonder where your sacrifice is, for what could you possibly give to God that would be worthy of him? The most precious and costly sacrifice that God demands . . . is *you!*

And one of the most important ways you can give yourself to God is by coming every Sunday morning to worship him with his people. This is not the only thing God requires you to give him in the church, but it's the most important one.

CHAPTER 4

The Church Is Your Mother

THE CHURCH IS ALSO your Mother.

In Galatians 4:26, Paul says, speaking of the Church: "the Jerusalem above is free, *which is the mother of us all.*" Paul is contrasting first-century Israel, which rejected Jesus, with the first-century Church. We know that the Jerusalem above is the Church from Revelation 21:2, where we read: "Then I, John, saw the holy city, New Jerusalem, coming down out of heaven from God, prepared as a bride adorned for her husband."

The early church fathers, who interpreted the Bible in the same way as St. Paul, also called the Church "Mother." Most famously, St. Cyprian said, around the year 250: "You cannot have God for your Father if you do not have the Church for your Mother." But even John Calvin, the great Reformer, wrote: "For those to whom he [God] is Father the church may also be Mother."

So, the Church is the Mother of every Christian. How so?

First, every Christian is born in the "womb" of the Church. It is within the context of our Mother Church that we receive the things of God that sustain our spiritual life. The Word of God, which brings life, was written to the Church, for the Church, and by the Church. The Church is the natural environment of the Bible and the place where it is guarded and dispensed.

Undoubtedly, it was someone in the Church who first led you to Jesus. This was probably your earthly mother and father, but even if it wasn't, it was someone who himself had been raised by the Church.

We are born into the Church at our baptism,[1] for it is then that we are brought into the divine life of Jesus Christ and made a member of both him and his Church. When we emerge from the baptismal waters, it is like passing out of the womb, through the birth canal, and into the new world of Christ.

Second, we are cared for by the Church. Every good mother cares for her children. She feeds and clothes them, helps them in times of trouble, and heals them. And so, your heavenly Mother prepares your spiritual food every day as well. Your Mother feeds you with the Word of God and sets it before you several times a day.

Unfortunately, some of us children are like earthly kids who rush out the door to play with their friends and say, "Sorry, Mom, I'm too busy to eat!" Or we eat the spiritual junk food that the world offers.

Your Mother carefully sets the table every Lord's Day and on it places the Bread of Life and the Living Water, the Body and Blood of Jesus Christ. And she desires to wean you off the spiritual milk that is for spiritual infants and give you the mature food of Christ and his house.

Your mother heals you. She changes your diaper so you don't wallow in your own filth. She takes care of your boo-boos. And she takes you to the doctor when you need it.

Your Mother the Church also helps heal you, for she brings you to the Great Physician himself, Jesus Christ. He is the one who healed all who were sick in the Gospels, and he is the one who will heal your soul when it is sick or broken. Your mother soothes your injuries, providing love and comfort when you are weak. The

---

1. I realize that not all Christians have the same understanding of the nature of baptism. But the early Church believed that baptism was the initiation into the life of the Church. This is also the belief of most Christians today, including Roman Catholics, Orthodox Christians, Anglicans, Lutherans, Presbyterians, and others.

mother is the one to whom you can tell your fears, the spiritual darknesses, and the monsters that scare us to death.

Your Mother prays for you. St. Augustine was a notorious evildoer when younger. But his mother, Monica, prayed for him for many years and prayed him back to spiritual health. And so, the Church prays for you.

Third, mothers teach their children. They tell them right from wrong from an early age. They tell them the facts of life. And they teach them that if you do these things, she and your father are pleased and you'll be blessed in these things, but if you do those things, your mother and father will be displeased, and you'll be hurt by those things. They teach you lifelong habits, teaching as much by example as by word.

The Church also instructs her children. After you've been born into the household of God, you need to be instructed. The Church has many means of teaching her children: we should attend to as many as possible:

- adult and children's Sunday school
- being attentive to the liturgy and sermon
- spiritual conversations with other Christians
- Bible reading and meditation

Mothers read to their children. Every time you hear a Bible lesson read in the Church: your Mother is reading you one of the family stories!

We learn from our Mother by example: this is why we look at the lives of Bible characters and the lives of the saints, including the ones who walk among us in the world today.

We learn obedience from our Mother. This is all-important, and it only hurts the children when they won't listen to the voice of their mother. Even Jesus, especially Jesus, learned obedience as the perfect Son.

Children, you may have noticed, need to be civilized. Just as women civilize us men, mothers civilize their children. The Church, as our Mother, civilizes us. For "civilization" comes from the Latin word for "citizen" or "city," and the Church trains us to live in the City of God.

This civilizing takes place through the godly habits the Church teaches us, not just attending worship on Sunday morning, but also how to read and meditate on the Scriptures, how to love, how to tell time with the Church year, and much more.

And a mother must sometimes say no to her children and their desires, lest they become spoiled and selfish.

Fourth, mothers protect and give their lives for their children. They drive away all predators and those who might hurt their children. In the same way, the Church protects her children.

Finally, mothers love their children. They exist to serve their children, and they willingly, joyfully give their lives for their children. They easily forgive their children their many wrongs. They hug and they hold their children.

It's no different with the Church.

CHAPTER 5
The Church Is Your Family

THE CHURCH IS THE Family of God—*your* Family. It's the way God intends to relate to men and the way he intends Christians to relate to each other.

The original Family of God is the Holy Trinity: the Father, the Son, and the Holy Spirit. But out of God's love, he desired to bring man into his Family. One way this communion with God is portrayed is the way we've already explored: the Church as the Body and Bride of Christ.

But our relationship with God as the people of God is also spoken of as a process of adoption. This is extraordinarily good news! God chose us, unlovable as we were, to be part of his Family.

I'll never forget a student I once had named Stephanie. She was a chubby ten-year-old girl, outwardly smiling from ear to ear but inwardly a bundle of wiggling nerves. She had such a sunny disposition that we called her "Moonbeam"—that and the fact that she thought she was a child of the sixties.

One day, at recess, I noticed her walking around the perimeter of the school fence, with her sunny face setting and eclipsed by some inner darkness. When I asked her what the matter was, she explained that she just found out that she was adopted. She was worried that she wasn't really her parents' daughter and that she didn't really belong to them.

Immediately, it occurred to me what the remedy was for her darkness. I told her that adoption was a wonderful thing and, that far from meaning that she didn't really belong to her family, it meant that her father and mother loved her so much that they chose her to live with them and be their child.

I told Stephanie that this was the way God worked with us. We were not his children; none of us were lovely or worthy of adoption. But he came to us and made us his children. And as his children, he has made us heirs of the richest kingdom ever known: the Kingdom of heaven.

Christians are those adopted into the Family of God. But none of us is a part of the Family of God directly: none of us can be the eternal and divine Son of God. But we do become the children of God when God adopts us into his Family, which means becoming a part of Jesus Christ and his Body.

Historically, Christians have most commonly understood this adoption to take place at our baptism, when God sovereignly reaches down and initiates a covenant relationship with us. At baptism, a Christian is made a child of God, a member of Christ (meaning his Church), and an inheritor of his Kingdom.

Regardless of your view of baptism, the Bible teaches that you must be adopted into the Family of God. By nature, we are born into the family of Adam and inherit sin and death. But out of love, God adopts us and makes us his children—if we have a relationship with him through his Son.

Think of how becoming a Christian and part of God's Church is like being adopted into a family. First, God chooses you and places you into his Family. He gives you his name, for you are called a Christian. Traditionally, at baptism the child to be baptized is given his "Christian" name, but he also has his new "family" name placed on him: the name of the Father, the Son, and the Holy Spirit. Because of this, we have the incredible privilege of calling God "Father"!

After you were adopted, God begins to treat you, just like an adoptive earthly parent, as if you were truly his own child. This means that you not only have the rights of being a member of God's Family but also the responsibilities. To live in your parents' house means not only that you have to live by their rules but also that you are blessed to be a partaker of their family life.

Why do parents make rules for their children and households? To train them in ways that will lead to their greater health and glory, and to protect them from evil and harm. The same is true in the house of God, the Church. This is where Christians learn how to live in God's Kingdom in such a way that they please their Father in heaven, are blessed by him, and are delivered from sin and its terrible consequences.

Third, living in your parents' house, you learn how to do life. The same is true of the Church. But while we "graduate" from our nuclear family when we're eighteen or twenty-one, we never graduate from God's Family, the Church, because it is the Family of families. When Christians leave the Church, where is the house of God for them? Nature? The secular world? The Church continually teaches us how to live like Christians, which means, primarily, to live in love for God and others. But this is hard to do when you don't actually spend much time living with God and other Christians in God's household and Family.

Earthly parents share their lives with their children, including not only their houses but also their food, their work, their play, and their time. They share, most of all, *themselves*. It's no different in the house of God. For in his house, the Church, God clothes us with his Son and his righteousness (as well as the armor of God); feeds us by his Word, sacrament, and fellowship; participates in a life with us; and does his work of ministry through us.

Wouldn't it be strange (and unhealthy) if a child claimed to love his parents but disobeyed them, ran away from home, never visited, never ate with them, never spoke with them, and only showed up when he needed something?

CHAPTER 6

You Are Your Tribe

You may have noticed a funny thing about growing up in a family: you end up sounding and acting a lot like your parents!

It used to mystify me how I learned to speak English. "Man," I thought, "Mom and Dad must have spent a lot of time teaching me!"

Of course, they didn't. I speak English because my parents spoke English. I grew up as a Christian because my parents are Christians. And I love reading and learning because my parents loved reading and learning. I grew up having a large vocabulary, being a good speller, and having a good understanding of the proper pronunciation of English words. But there was one word I was saying in an uncommon way—the word "advertisement."

Most Americans pronounce the word with the accent on the first syllable. But my mother put the accent on the second syllable. The first time someone laughed at my pronunciation, I was both embarrassed and mystified. But it goes to show you how much we're influenced by the people around us.

The truth is: you become like the people you hang out with.

You *are* your tribe or family. This is the idea of *corporate personality* I introduced in chapter 1.

Most people who have ever lived knew this. A Roman was proud to be a Roman, an Athenian would be proud to be an

Athenian, and Christians have thought of themselves first and foremost as being disciples of Jesus Christ and members of his Church.

Not only this: most of what we think, do, and say is because we've been shaped by the people around us, especially our family.

The Church is the Family of God—*your* Family, if you're a Christian. God has put you in this Family, as one of his children, so that you can learn to love and receive love. It's in God's Family, the Church, that we are shaped and molded in the likeness of Jesus Christ.

The Church is not just a social club that has meetings once a week: it's a culture, and it produces a culture around it. A culture is an entire way of life, a way of understanding the world, and a way of looking and valuing things. It's all-encompassing.

The culture of the Church is often very different from the culture of the world.

It has very different ideas about whether unborn children are really humans made in the image of God or just lumps of tissue, whether we should take someone's life at the end of life because they're suffering, whether marriage is between a man and a woman, whether sex outside of marriage is sinful, whether life is about loving God and others or serving self, and many other things.

If you're a Christian and you look honestly at your own life, I'll bet you'll notice two very important things.

First, if you're like most of us, you became a Christian under the influence of someone who thought being part of a church was very important.

Second, when you've lived your life without being part of a church, you begin to think and act a lot more like the culture around you than you do a Christian. Often, we speak of this process as becoming more "worldly."

This is a truth that even non-Christians find is true: you are the company you keep. King Solomon explained it this way: "He who walks with wise men will be wise, but the companion of fools will be destroyed" (Prov 13:20). St. Paul puts it this way: "Do not be deceived: evil company corrupts good habits'" (1 Cor 15:33).

A Christian who spends most of his life with those who don't love God inevitably begins to live more like someone who doesn't love God.

But the opposite is also true: someone who spends a lot of time with godly men and women will end up thinking, talking, and living like them.

More than this, the kind of people you choose to surround yourself tells a lot about what you truly care about. If you care about gaming, you seek out and choose to spend time with gamers. If you like partying, you go to parties and find like-minded people. And if you love God, you go to a church and spend time with the people there, sharing your life with them.

Who you choose to spend time with tells you a lot about what you really value most in life, just like what you spend most of your free time doing tells you the same.

We were made for community, since God is a communion of three Persons, and he's adopted us into his Family. It's inescapable that each of us will be profoundly shaped by the tribes we join. There's a reason that skaters look like skaters, bikers look like bikers, nerds look like nerds, and Goths look like Goths. While there are too many Christians (who belong to too many other tribes) for us all to look alike on the outside, Christians who go to church tend to act a lot alike.

"It is not good for man to live alone," God said to Adam. And so, he created Eve for Adam and created the human family. Just as it's not good for a man to live with evil men, it's not good for men to live alone, either. It's not just that God created us to live together, it's also that in order for love to live and flourish, we must live together. Love, in its very essence, is a giving of self to someone else for his good, something we can't give and receive if we don't live together.

It's pretty obvious to most of us that we have a huge problem with depression in our culture today. Most of us know many people who are depressed. While depression probably has multiple causes, it seems as if the primary cause is the way we've chosen to live alone. More specifically, divorcing ourselves from each other is painful, and a natural response to this kind of pain is what we call depression.

Think about the many ways we divorce ourselves from one another and what it's doing to us. Most painfully, husbands and wives divorce each other, including a very large number of Christian husbands and wives. We move away from our families, not only moving out of the house at eighteen but moving away from family and friends when we go to college and moving halfway across the country (or further) when we get the jobs we so desperately want.

Churches, the nation, neighborhoods, schools, and families are all weaker than they used to be as communities that bind us together.

To make matters worse, we spend a lot of time by ourselves playing games or binge-watching fictional people on TV. While social media appears to connect us with people, it usually does just the opposite. In fact, it's a major factor in depression for many people.

You are who you hang out with: you are your tribe.
And the Christian tribe is the Church.

CHAPTER 7

The Bible and the Church Always Go Together

THE BIBLE AND THE Church always go together. This is difficult for modern Christians to see, but I hope to help you see it by showing you two things:

1. how we got the Bible
2. what the Bible says about the Church

HOW WE GOT THE BIBLE

Most Christian don't know much about how we got the Bible. Once we know this, however, we can more easily see why I said that you can't have the Bible without the Church (and vice versa).

So, how did we get the Bible?

The Bible was originally written over a period of about 1,500 years. The Old Testament books were written from the time of Moses (a little later than 1500 BC) until the time of Malachi (around 400 BC). The New Testament books were written over a much shorter period of time, from the 40s AD until sometime near the end of the first century.

THE BIBLE AND THE CHURCH ALWAYS GO TOGETHER

After the books of the Bible were originally written, however, how did they become the Bible? It's helpful to think of the formation of the Bible in five stages:

1. *Writing*—Under the inspiration of the Holy Spirit, each writer of the Bible wrote one or more of the books of the Bible. Almost all of the Old Testament was originally written in Hebrew, and the New Testament was written in koine ("common") Greek.

   When the Bible was written, it was always written in the context of the Church—either the Old Testament Church, which was Israel, or the New Testament Church. For example, the book of Genesis was written by Moses for the people of God at the time of the giving of the Law and the deliverance of Israel from Egypt.

2. *Transmission*—After the original manuscript was written, each book of the Bible had to be faithfully transcribed, or copied, so it could be passed down to other generations and circulated more widely. This copying of the Scriptures was done in the context of the Church: for most of history, no one would have had the Scriptures except the Church and Church leaders.

3. *Canonization*—At some point, the Church had to confirm or ratify which books of the Bible were truly inspired.

   The Church played an important role in determining the canon of the Bible, but this role must be correctly understood. On the one hand, the divine nature of the books of the Bible was recognized by the Church before the Church ever officially compiled a list of canonical books. On the other hand, in the fourth century, especially, the Church began to officially declare the canon of the New Testament that had already been accepted unofficially.

   What's most important to know is that if there were no Church, we would not have an agreed-upon Bible today.

4. *Translation*—Early on, the Church translated the Bible into vernacular or local languages. Unlike the Koran, which is theoretically only the Koran in Arabic, Christians believe they truly have the Word of God in the Holy Scriptures, even when

translated. Until the twentieth century, the Bible was translated and published by the Church.
5. *Interpretation* – Even though you can and should read your Bible, it needs to be interpreted. God has given special authority to the Church to guard the Scriptures by faithfully interpreting them. Jesus gave his authority to his apostles, such as St. Paul, who passed on this authority to men like Titus and Timothy.

So, this is how we got the Bible that you read today.

Up until the nineteenth century, the majority of Christians would only have *heard* the Word of God in Church, and not read it at home. They understood that the Bible and the Church always go together.

WHAT THE BIBLE SAYS ABOUT THE CHURCH

There's a second reason why you can't have the Bible without the Church: what the Bible itself says about the Church.

The assumption of the writers of the books of the Bible is that the Word of God is inseparable from the people of God. As we've already seen, the Bible was written by the Church, for the Church. It was also copied and translated by the Church, and the Church has the authority to interpret it today.

Imagine, for a moment, that you lived in Israel at the time of Moses, and you wanted to know what God had to say. No one in Israel would have ever thought that he could be a good Israelite and not live as part of Israel and its religious culture.

To be an Israelite, one had to be circumcised (or be a female in the household of a man who was), live by God's Law as proclaimed and taught by the "Church" leaders, attend the three annual feasts, offer up appropriate sacrifices, etc. To be an Israelite, you had to be a member of Israel, God's people.

No one in the Old Testament who was not part of the nation of Israel and did not live as an Israelite would ever have said, "I can have a good relationship with God without being a part of Israel."

THE NEW TESTAMENT IS ALL ABOUT THE CHURCH

What about the New Testament?

The truth is that the New Testament is all about the Church, and after the establishment of the Church after Christ's ascension, every book of the New Testament assumes that individual Christians are members of a local church—*every book*.

The Gospels are, of course, about the life of Jesus Christ in the flesh. We've already talked at length about how the Church is now the Body of Christ on earth.

But what about the rest of the New Testament?

If you read the book of Acts, written by St. Luke, you'll quickly discover that the book is all about the Church. More specifically, it's about what Jesus Christ, now ascended to heaven, continues to do and to teach through his Church. On the Day of Pentecost, Jesus filled his Body with his Spirit, and the Church became the living presence of Jesus on earth.

This is why throughout the rest of the book of Acts, the apostles teach the things Jesus taught and do the things Jesus did. St. Stephen dies in the way Jesus did, forgiving his murderers.

The apostles perform the same kind of miracles as Jesus did, even raising people from the dead (for example, Eutyches in chapter 20). It's clear that the book is about Jesus Christ continuing to live through his Church.

The book of Acts is unique, but most of the New Testament is made up of books that are letters. Let's look at these letters by beginning with a simple question: to whom were the letters written?

There are twenty-one letters in the New Testament.

The following letters are all written directly to churches: Romans, 1 and 2 Corinthians, Galatians, Ephesians, Philippians, Colossians, and 1 and 2 Thessalonians. That makes nine of the twenty-one letters we can easily see are written to churches.

What about the others?

Let's deal with them in order.

1 Timothy, *2 Timothy*, and *Titus* are easy to deal with. Even though they're not written to churches—they're written to *church leaders!* Timothy and Titus were among the first bishops, elders and rulers, over a group of churches. Each of these three letters is all about how Timothy or Titus should govern the church, including the qualifications for elders and deacons, the church leaders.

While Paul wrote *Philemon* primarily to an individual slave owner, and not a church, if you read Paul's entire greeting, he makes clear that he's also writing to "the church in your [Philemon's] house" (verse 2). It appears as if Paul wants the entire church to hear the letter and help Philemon do the right thing.

There are several places in the letter to the *Hebrews* where the author makes it clear that he's writing about the church. For example, in 12:22–23, the author writes: "But you have come to Mount Zion and to the city of the living God, the *heavenly Jerusalem*, to an innumerable company of angels, to the general *assembly* and *church* of the firstborn who are registered in heaven." The words "assembly" and "church" clearly refer to the Church, while "heavenly Jerusalem" is another name given to the Church (see Rev 21).

In 13:7, the author writes: "Remember those who rule over you, who have spoken the word of God to you, whose faith follow, considering the outcome of their conduct." In this context, he's clearly speaking about faithful rulers in the local churches.

Most clearly and significantly, the writer of the letter to the Hebrews says: "And let us consider one another in order to stir up love and good works, *not forsaking the assembling of ourselves together,* as is the manner of some, but exhorting one another, and so much the more as you see the Day approaching" (10:25). The author is writing to a church with leaders. In this church, some of the members have given up being a part of the church's worship, which the author considers something to be corrected.

James wrote his letter to the twelve tribes. Most scholars believe this means Jewish Christian churches, for it would make no sense for James to send his letter to each individual Jewish Christian. James speaks of how to treat poor people in the assembly or church (2:2). He speaks of teachers in the churches to whom he is writing (3:1). James also assumes there are elders in the local church to whom people should come for healing, anointing, and prayer (5:13–14).

Peter, in his first letter, writes to the "pilgrims of the Dispersion in Pontus, Galatia, Cappadocia, Asia, and Bithynia" (1:1). While he doesn't mention the word "church," the only way the letter could be circulated to the Christians in these regions would be if Peter were writing to churches. Notice, too, that Peter is writing to a region where Paul also wrote a letter: Galatia.

Peter clearly thinks that his audience is the church, the community of God's people, for he tells his audience "you are a chosen generation, a royal priesthood, a holy nation, His own special people, that you may proclaim the praises of Him who called you out of darkness into His marvelous light; who once were not a people but are now the people of God" (2:9–10).

In his second letter, Peter talks about false prophets who arose among the people (2:1), and he's writing to the same people as in his first letter (3:2), so everything we said about 1 Peter applies to 2 Peter.

John's first letter doesn't spell out to whom he is writing, as do his second and third letters. But he is writing to those he considers his little children, and we know that John ministered to churches in Asia Minor (modern-day Turkey). He is obviously writing to a large group of people, whom he refers to as "little children," "fathers," and "young men" (2:12–14).

2 John is written by the elder to the elect lady and her children, the elect lady being the church (1:1).

3 John is, once again, written by the elder. Even though the letter is written to an individual, Gaius, John is clearly writing to Gaius in the context of the church, which he references in verses 6 and 9–10.

Jude makes clear in verses 3–4 that he's writing to a community of believers. He speaks of their "common salvation," as well as those who have "crept in" to it.

This leaves only John's *Revelation*. Revelation is not a letter but is written in the genre of apocalypse, which speaks of earth-changing events. John clearly writes his Revelation to churches, for he says that he's writing to: "the seven churches which are in Asia" (1:4). It is these seven churches to whom he has written the entire Apocalypse, as well as specific messages in chapters 1 and 2. The "Asia" here is Asia Minor, the place where John served as a kind of bishop over several churches.

The Revelation ends with a bang—and with the Church! For, in the end, Revelation is about Jesus Christ marrying his Bride, the Church.

We've discussed this earlier, in chapter 1, but if you want to look at the passages again, you'll find them in 19:7–9 and 21:2, 9–11.

You see, then, that the entire New Testament is about the Church and is written to the Church and individual churches.

You can't have the Bible without the Church, and you can't have the Church without the Bible. You can't have the Word of God without the people of God, and you can't have the people of God without the Word of God.

CHAPTER 8

The Church Is Filled with Sinners Just Like You

When I talk to people about why they no longer are part of a church, there are two top reasons I hear (even if the real reason is often something different):

1. The church is full of hypocrites.
2. The church hurt me.

Both of these reasons make me sad. I'm sad whenever we hurt one another, but I'm even sadder that out of such hurt people make decisions that hurt them even more—especially the decision to give up on the Church.

You shouldn't give up on God or his Church because of the people in it.

For who are the people in churches? God's answer is that they're *redeemed sinners*—just like you!

First, they're sinners. A sinner is someone who disobeys what God commands and loves and trusts himself more than God. A sinner is someone made in the image of God who lives for himself as if God doesn't exist and who falls far short of what God desires.

And all of us are sinners: you, me, your pastor, the Christians who have hurt you and whom you've hurt, and everyone who has ever lived (except Jesus).

But Christians are also *redeemed* sinners. There's only been one perfect and sinless man, and that was Jesus Christ, who also happens to be God. Every Christian you have ever met or ever will meet is a sinner. It means that every Christian, at times, will act selfishly and in ways that hurt other people. Every Christian fails to love, to varying degrees.

But being a Christian also means that God has saved or redeemed that person. Through the sacrifice of God's perfect Son, who took on human nature, died on the cross, and rose from the grave, God has saved men.

So, you won't find any perfect Christians, and you won't find any perfect churches.

In fact, if you do find a perfect church—do us all a favor. Don't join it: you'll ruin it!

Saying that you don't go to church because it's filled with sinners doesn't really make sense, does it? If we all had that attitude, there would be no churches at all. It's like saying I will only stay married if my spouse is perfect.

Thank God that he doesn't have that attitude! Jesus didn't come to live and die for the righteous: he came for sinners! He came for the hypocrites and the prostitutes, the tax collectors and the outcasts, and for every kind of sinner that was willing to turn to him and give him their lives.

I don't want to minimize how much we Christians can hurt one another. But don't let the hypocrisy or other sins of your brothers and sisters in Christ keep you from church.

The Church is where we go to find forgiveness—and to give it. Jesus Christ, whose Body the Church is, was all about forgiveness. And he's entrusted to us, the Church, his ministry of forgiveness and reconciliation (2 Cor 5:18).

If you leave God's Church because people have wronged you, then it just might be true that you haven't really forgiven them or sought reconciliation. But seeking forgiveness, and giving it, is the very essence of the Christian life.

How important is forgiveness?

God sent his Son in the world to forgive us of our sins.

Jesus died an excruciating death on the cross to forgive us of our sins.

Forgiveness is at the very center of the Lord's Prayer, the *one* prayer Jesus left us to pray.

So important is forgiveness that Jesus, when he gave his disciples the Lord's Prayer, added: "But if you do not forgive men their trespasses, neither will your Father forgive your trespasses" (Matt 6:15).

JESUS "WENT TO CHURCH" WITH SINNERS IN A CORRUPT CHURCH

WWJD was a popular slogan years ago—"What would Jesus do?"

When it comes to dealing with a church filled with sinners, hypocrites, and people who hurt us, we know exactly what Jesus did—he went to church!

Jesus attended the synagogue every Sabbath day. Can you imagine what he experienced when he went? He worshiped in the synagogue and temple, knowing exactly how corrupt the Church of his day had become and knowing exactly how much those in the Church would mistreat him.

Think of it: Jesus endured every time a Jewish rabbi or teacher led the people away from God by false teaching, acted like a hypocrite, or denied Jesus.

Worse than that, when Jesus preached his very first sermon in his hometown of Nazareth, the people wanted to kill him! (Luke 4:16–30).

Many of the Jewish leaders were corrupt, and many even wanted to kill Jesus. Jesus experienced greater hypocrisy than you ever will, and he was hurt by church members more than you ever will be. And yet he attended all of the Jewish feasts, offered up all of the required sacrifices with God's people, and kept worshiping in the Jewish synagogues.

HOW TO SEEK FORGIVENESS IN THE CHURCH

Jesus left us a process to deal with our sins when we commit them against each other as Christians, and it involves the local church.

When Jesus told his disciples how much God loves finding lost sinners and reminding them of the dangers of unforgiveness, he gave them a way to deal with a brother who has sinned against you. The passage is Matthew 18:15–17, where Jesus says:

> Moreover if your brother sins against you, go and tell him his fault between you and him alone. If he hears you, you have gained your brother. But if he will not hear, take with you one or two more, that "by the mouth of two or three witnesses every word may be established." And if he refuses to hear them, tell it to the church. But if he refuses even to hear the church, let him be to you like a heathen and a tax collector.

The first step in resolving a problem where one Christian brother has hurt another, Jesus says, is to go to the brother you believe has sinned against you and tell him his fault. Ideally, the one who has sinned will acknowledge his sin, ask for forgiveness, and receive it from the one who was wronged. This is the way God has acted with repentant sinners.

But what if your brother won't listen? Maybe you've imagined a wrong, or maybe he can't see it or won't acknowledge it. Maybe both of you are to blame. What do you do?

Jesus says you should go with other brothers or sisters. That is, bring into the process others who are witnesses of the wrong so that you can make your case more forcefully and establish it more surely. In many cases, one who's sinned will feel compelled to confess and ask forgiveness.

What if the brother, in the face of evidence from two witnesses or more, still won't confess? The last step, Jesus says, is to tell your wrong to the Church. Why would Jesus say this? Why not just leave it at the second step? Because the Church is the Body of Christ and has the authority of Jesus himself. It's in the Church, especially, that forgiveness is given.

Churches with historic liturgies, including Roman Catholics, Orthodox Christians, Anglicans, Lutherans, and others, have a confession of sin as part of their worship service. In such churches, the minister pronounces a public absolution, as a representative of Jesus, of the forgiveness of sins.

So how would bringing your grievance to the church look? Most likely, it would mean taking your problem to your pastor, as the leader of your local congregation and a representative of God to the people.

If you're not in a church, the possibilities for forgiveness are greatly diminished. The public pronunciation of the forgiveness of sins that's in the absolution, the worship service, the hymns, and the sermon are no longer a part of your life.

So maybe you've walked away from the Church because you've been hurt by someone else's sin.

Here are some questions to ask yourself.

1. When you were hurt, did you seek the biblical means of reconciliation?
2. Did you bring two or three brothers or sisters as witnesses, if you sought reconciliation, but the other person wasn't willing?
3. Did you involve your pastor or elders?
4. Have you forgiven those who wronged you?
5. If you've done numbers 1–4, then you should return to your local church in peace. If you haven't, then you should seek reconciliation.

CHAPTER 9

Don't Excommunicate Yourself

EXCOMMUNICATION USED TO BE a big deal.

Way back in the 1070s, a very important pope, Gregory VII (also known as Hildebrand), had a dispute with a very important emperor, Henry IV, the Holy Roman Emperor. The dispute was over who had the authority to appoint bishops and other church leaders.

In 1075, Henry installed the bishop of Milan without the consent of Pope Gregory. A suspicious assassination attempt was made on the pope's life, and Henry called a German church meeting, where his church leaders rejected any commitment to the pope. In response, Gregory VII declared Henry IV excommunicated. This so undermined Henry's position that in 1076 he made a pilgrimage to meet the pope at his castle in Canossa.

The pope refused to allow Henry in to talk until he had first shown repentance. Henry then played the part of the penitent, wearing a hair shirt and walking barefoot in the snow for three days. In the end, the pope let Henry in, deeming that he was truly penitent.

So, what's the big deal about excommunication? Why would this great emperor care that the pope had excommunicated him?

Excommunication technically means that a Christian is refused the right to "communicate," that is, to partake of the bread and wine, by which God gives the body and blood of Jesus Christ, in the Lord's Supper. This is the ultimate form of church discipline, and one used very sparingly. More than just a denial of the right to take Communion, excommunication also meant that you were no longer a member in good standing in the local church.

Too many Christians today, this all seems very foreign. But historically, from the very beginning of the Church in the first century, Christians believed that partaking of Jesus Christ in the Lord's Supper was the most important thing a Christian could do. This is because they believed that Jesus is truly present in his Supper in a special way.

When, however, a Christian decides he doesn't need the Church, he has, effectively, excommunicated himself. The Church is the only place where you can get the Lord's Supper and be blessed by him in this special way. To excommunicate yourself also means that you've effectively removed yourself from all of the ways in which God specially blesses his people through being a member of a local church.

THE IMPORTANCE OF TAKING COMMUNION

Let me explain the importance of being excommunicated in two ways, both in terms of the Lord's Supper and in terms of being a part of the local church.

Jesus certainly believed that his Supper was essential for all Christians to partake of. He gave his Supper to his disciples on the night before he gave his life on the cross for you and for me. He presented his Supper as being the true Passover meal, which all of God's people in the Old Testament were required to eat if they were to be saved.

Paul also records Jesus' words as they had been passed down to him:

> For I received from the Lord that which I also delivered to you: that the Lord Jesus on the same night in which he was betrayed took bread; and when He had given thanks, He broke it and said, "Take, eat; this is My body which is broken for you; do this in remembrance of Me." In the

> same manner He also took the cup after supper, saying, "This cup is the new covenant in My blood. This do, as often as you drink it, in remembrance of Me." For as often as you eat this bread and drink this cup, you proclaim the Lord's death till He comes. (1 Cor 11:23-26)

Jesus commanded that his disciples partake of the Passover as a continual participation in him and his sacrifice. Paul obviously felt that the Lord's Supper was very important—so important that he recorded the exact words that were passed down to him, the same words that Jesus left his disciples and which the Gospel writers recorded.

In 1 Corinthians, Paul shows us how important he felt the Lord's Supper was in two other ways. First, he gives instructions on how it is to be conducted, assuming that the local church is practicing the Lord's Supper regularly. Some in the church in Corinth were not partaking of the Lord's Supper in the right way. Here is the seriousness with which Apostle Paul took the Lord's Supper:

> Therefore whoever eats this bread or drinks this cup of the Lord in an unworthy manner will be guilty of the body and blood of the Lord. But let a man examine himself, and so let him eat of the bread and drink of the cup. For he who eats and drinks in an unworthy manner eats and drinks judgment to himself, not discerning the Lord's body. For this reason many are weak and sick among you, and many sleep. (1 Cor 11:27-30)

Paul says that if anyone eats the bread or drinks the cup of the Lord's Supper unworthily, he is guilty of the body and blood of Jesus! Paul obviously thought that in some way, the very body and blood of Jesus were connected to the Lord's Supper. For this reason, not only should all Christians regularly partake of the Lord's Supper: they should also partake of it in a worthy manner.

Paul believes that those who partake of the Lord's Supper in an unworthy manner do so because they don't discern the Lord's Body. This probably means two things. It especially means that they don't recognize that Jesus is present in his Supper. But it also means that those who eat unworthily are thinking only about themselves, and not about the whole church of which they are a part.

Paul also believes that because some in the church in Corinth are eating unworthily, not seeing that Jesus was in his meal, they were being judged by God and getting sick and even dying! When Paul says "many sleep," he's using a figure of speech that means "dying."

And so, the first reason to not excommunicate yourself by not belonging to a church and living with it is that in so doing you are barring yourself from eating the Lord's Supper, which Jesus not only commands but by which he promises to bless his people with his presence.

The only place you can partake of the Lord's Supper is in the local church!

THE IMPORTANCE OF COMMUNION WITH THE CHURCH

Someone who has "excommunicated" himself from the Church has not only cut himself off from Jesus as he comes in his Supper, but has also cut himself off from the spiritual life that God gives us through life in the Church.

Often, we think of Christian spirituality as my individual, interior, invisible relationship with Jesus Christ. But this is only a partial truth.

A better definition of Christian spirituality is this: "spirituality is the life of Christ communicated to the Body of Christ by the Spirit of Christ." As we discussed earlier, life in Christ means life in his Body, the Church.

It's only in the local church that you can receive the Lord's Supper.

It's only in the local church that you can hear God's Word authoritatively preached and taught.

It's only in the local church that the spiritual gifts you have can be truly exercised (see Romans 12, 1 Corinthians 12 and 14).

It's only in the local church that you can fully live out a community life together, forgiving and being forgiven.

CHAPTER 10

God Commands It!

THERE'S ONE FINAL REASON that every Christian must be a member of a local church: God commands it!

All of the other reasons require a little bit of thought in your head. This one only requires your heart.

If you say that you love him, then you must obey him. That's not difficult at all to understand. It's just that sometimes we don't want to obey God.

Obedience is at the heart of your relationship to God, so much so that we can say that you love God to the degree that you obey him and put his will before your own.

"Obedience" has almost become a dirty word among some Christians, as if God would never demand our obedience, or as if obedience is an unnecessary or even legalistic thing. But that's man speaking, and not God. The next time you wonder about the importance of obedience, just think of Jesus.

Jesus said that he came to do the will of the Father. In fact, he said, "My *food* is to do the will of Him who sent Me" (John 4:34).

Here's what St. Paul wrote about the importance of the Son's obedience to the Father: "being found in appearance as a man, He humbled Himself and became obedient to the point of death, even the death of the cross" (Phil 2:8).

When Jesus wrestled in the garden of Gethsemane, on the night before he died on the cross for you, he prayed that the Father would take the awful cup of suffering from him. But he also prayed: "nevertheless not My will, but Yours, be done" (Luke 22:42).

But obeying God in this matter of becoming a member of the Body of Christ is not just about obedience, as important as that is: it's about love. Jesus says, "If you love Me, keep My commandments" (John 14:15; see also 1 John 5:3 and 2 John 2:6).

God, throughout his written Word, assumes that his people are members of a church. We've seen the following:

1. The whole Church is the Bride of Christ, and Jesus has only one Bride, not two and a half billion brides.
2. The Church is the Body of Christ, of which each Christian is a member. This requires each Christian to be a member of a local church.
3. Each Christian is given spiritual gifts to build up the Body and not to build up himself. This requires you to be a member of a local church.
4. The Church is your Family, with leaders to help you grow in faith and love and in the image of Jesus Christ.
5. The Bible was formed and meant to be read, interpreted, and lived out in the context of the Church.
6. The Church is where you are fed the Word of God, disciplined and forgiven, corrected, and find your true identity.
7. The Church is the only place where you can receive the Lord's Supper.

But for those of you who want a Bible verse that directly says so, here you go!

"[L]et us consider one another in order to stir up love and good works, not forsaking the assembling of ourselves together, as is the manner of some" (Heb 10:24–25).

And so, God commands you to be a part of his people, his Church, the Body of his Son, and the Bride of Jesus Christ. I'm sure you have your reasons, but none of them trumps God's commandment and his desire to do you good through his Church.

Jesus once told a story about people who made excuses for not accepting his invitation to attend his Supper.

> Then He said to him, "A certain man gave a great supper and invited many, and sent his servant at supper time to say to those who were invited, 'Come, for all things are now ready.' But they all with one accord began to make excuses. The first said to him, 'I have bought a piece of ground, and I must go and see it. I ask you to have me excused.' And another said, 'I have bought five yoke of oxen, and I am going to test them. I ask you to have me excused.' Still another said, 'I have married a wife, and therefore I cannot come.' So that servant came and reported these things to his master. Then the master of the house, being angry, said to his servant, 'Go out quickly into the streets and lanes of the city, and bring in here the poor and the maimed and the lame and the blind.' And the servant said, 'Master, it is done as you commanded, and still there is room.' Then the master said to the servant, 'Go out into the highways and hedges, and compel them to come in, that my house may be filled. For I say to you that none of those men who were invited shall taste my supper.'" (Luke 14:16–24).

Don't be among those who make excuses for not becoming a part of a local church. Don't be among those who miss out on the blessing of God or who reject his will that you become a faithful member of a church.

Next Steps

GOD WANTS YOU TO be a member of a local church. What should you do next if you're not already a member of a local church?

1. JOIN A LOCAL CHURCH AND GET DEEPLY INVOLVED IN IT.

It may take time to find a good church, but don't let this become an excuse for not joining one. Becoming a faithful member of a local church is a process. It won't happen all at once, but you should be seeking to worship and serve the Lord more deeply week by week, in your chosen local church.

2. MAKE IT A PRIORITY TO GO EVERY LORD'S DAY, AS WELL AS TO OTHER WORSHIP SERVICES AND EVENTS.

Your local church, where God promises to meet with you and specially bless you, should be the center of your life. This will mean rearranging your schedule and giving up some things to be at the church worshiping and serving God, loving your brothers and sisters in Christ, and receiving their love.

Spend time with your church family, for they are also the Family of God and the primary way he comes to you to bless you.

3. FIND SOMEONE TO WALK WITH YOU.

Find someone from the local church who will hold you accountable for coming to church every week and who you can talk with about your journey.

4. DON'T BE ASHAMED.

It's hard to start going back to church, and it's natural to feel ashamed for not having gone. This is especially true if you're going back to a church where you used to attend.

But believe me: God is *delighted* that you're coming back into his house to live with him and worship him. If He's going to judge you, it's for *not* faithfully coming to his house when He's invited you—*not* for actually coming back!

You're something like the Prodigal Son. The father in that story was ecstatic that his lost son had returned, and he prepared a feast for him.

Most of your brothers and sisters will be as happy as God that you've come back to the church. They will welcome you with open arms. Yes, there may be a few who aren't very friendly or who even secretly judge you. But they'll be the minority, and they aren't the ones you should pay the most attention to.

So, come back to God today: come back into his holy Church.

For the Church is the Body and Bride of Jesus Christ.

The degree to which you love the Church, which is both the Bride and Body of Christ, is the degree to which you are loving Jesus: no more, no less.

www.ingramcontent.com/pod-product-compliance
Lightning Source LLC
Chambersburg PA
CBHW061515040426
42450CB00008B/1631